FILM HITS
AUDITION SONGS

FEMALE SINGERS

WISE PUBLICATIONS
PART OF THE MUSIC SALES GROUP
LONDON / NEW YORK / PARIS / SYDNEY / COPENHAGEN / BERLIN / MADRID / TOKYO

Published by
WISE PUBLICATIONS
14-15 Berners Street, London W1T 3LJ, UK.

Exclusive Distributors:
MUSIC SALES LIMITED
Distribution Centre, Newmarket Road,
Bury St Edmunds, Suffolk IP33 3YB, UK.
MUSIC SALES PTY LIMITED
20 Resolution Drive,
Caringbah, NSW 2229, Australia.

Order No. AM993410
ISBN 978-1-84772-535-6
This book © Copyright 2009 Wise Publications,
a division of Music Sales Limited.

Unauthorised reproduction of any part of this publication by any
means including photocopying is an infringement of copyright.

Music edited by Fiona Bolton.
Printed in the EU.

CD recorded, mixed and mastered by Jonas Persson
Backing tracks arranged by Paul Honey
Keyboard by Paul Honey
Guitars by Arthur Dick
Bass by Phil Mulford
Drums by Tim Goodyer

ANGEL *from* CITY OF ANGELS
SARAH MCLACHLAN
MUSIC PAGE 5 / CD TRACK 1

GOLDFINGER *from* GOLDFINGER
SHIRLEY BASSEY
MUSIC PAGE 10 / CD TRACK 2

I'M KISSING YOU *from* ROMEO + JULIET
DES'REE
MUSIC PAGE 15 / CD TRACK 3

LISTEN *from* DREAMGIRLS
BEYONCÉ
MUSIC PAGE 20 / CD TRACK 4

NINE TO FIVE *from* NINE TO FIVE
DOLLY PARTON
MUSIC PAGE 25 / CD TRACK 5

ONLY HOPE *from* A WALK TO REMEMBER
MANDY MOORE
MUSIC PAGE 30 / CD TRACK 6

PART OF YOUR WORLD *from* THE LITTLE MERMAID
JODI BENSON
MUSIC PAGE 34 / CD TRACK 7

RUN TO YOU *from* THE BODYGUARD
WHITNEY HOUSTON
MUSIC PAGE 41 / CD TRACK 8

TAKE MY BREATH AWAY *from* TOP GUN
BERLIN
MUSIC PAGE 46 / CD TRACK 9

THE WINNER TAKES IT ALL *from* MAMMA MIA!
ABBA/MERYL STREEP
MUSIC PAGE 50 / CD TRACK 10

Your Guarantee of Quality:
As publishers, we strive to produce every book
to the highest commercial standards.
The music has been freshly engraved and the book has
been carefully designed to minimise awkward page turns
and to make playing from it a real pleasure.
Particular care has been given to specifying acid-free,
neutral-sized paper made from pulps which have not been
elemental chlorine bleached.
This pulp is from farmed sustainable forests and was
produced with special regard for the environment.
Throughout, the printing and binding have been planned
to ensure a sturdy, attractive publication which should give
years of enjoyment.
If your copy fails to meet our high standards, please
inform us and we will gladly replace it.

www.musicsales.com

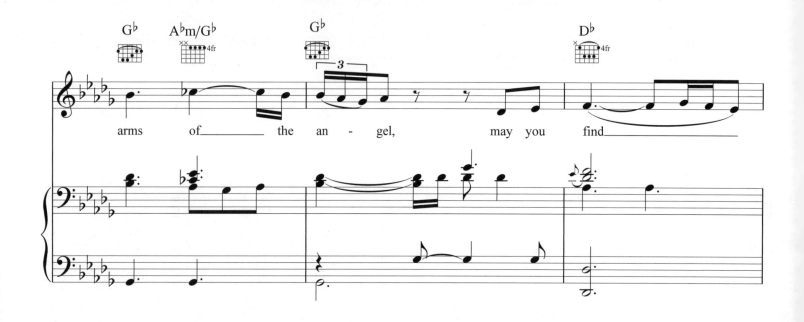
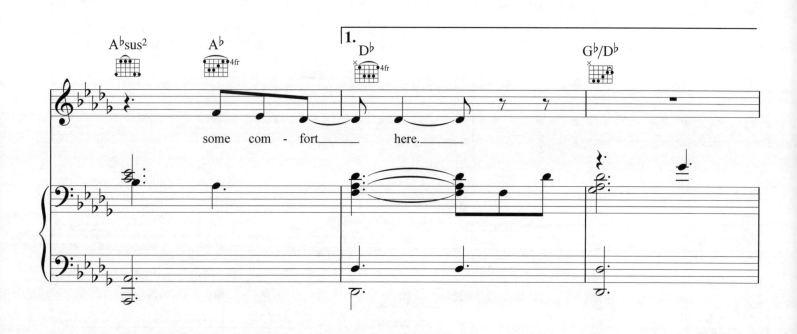
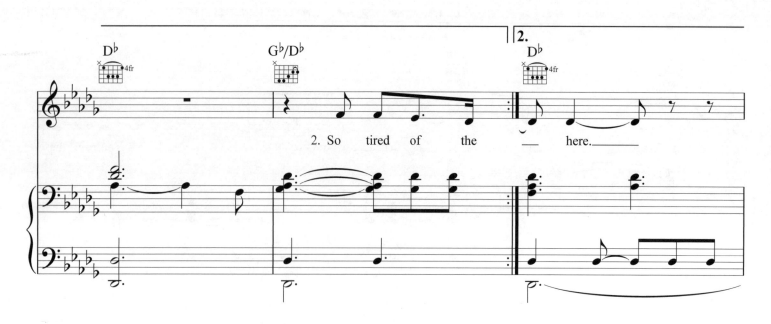

GOLDFINGER

WORDS BY LESLIE BRICUSSE & ANTHONY NEWLEY
MUSIC BY JOHN BARRY

I'M KISSING YOU

WORDS BY DES'REE
MUSIC BY DES'REE & TIM ATACK

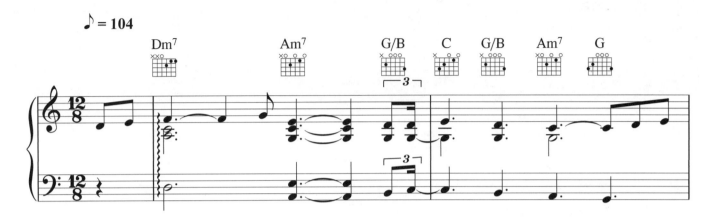
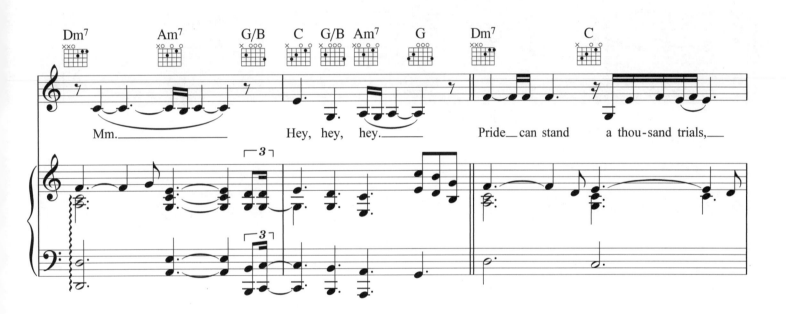

© Copyright 1998 Sony/ATV Music Publishing (UK) Limited (50%)/Love Lane Music (UK)/Westbury Music Consultants Limited (50%).
All Rights Reserved. International Copyright Secured.

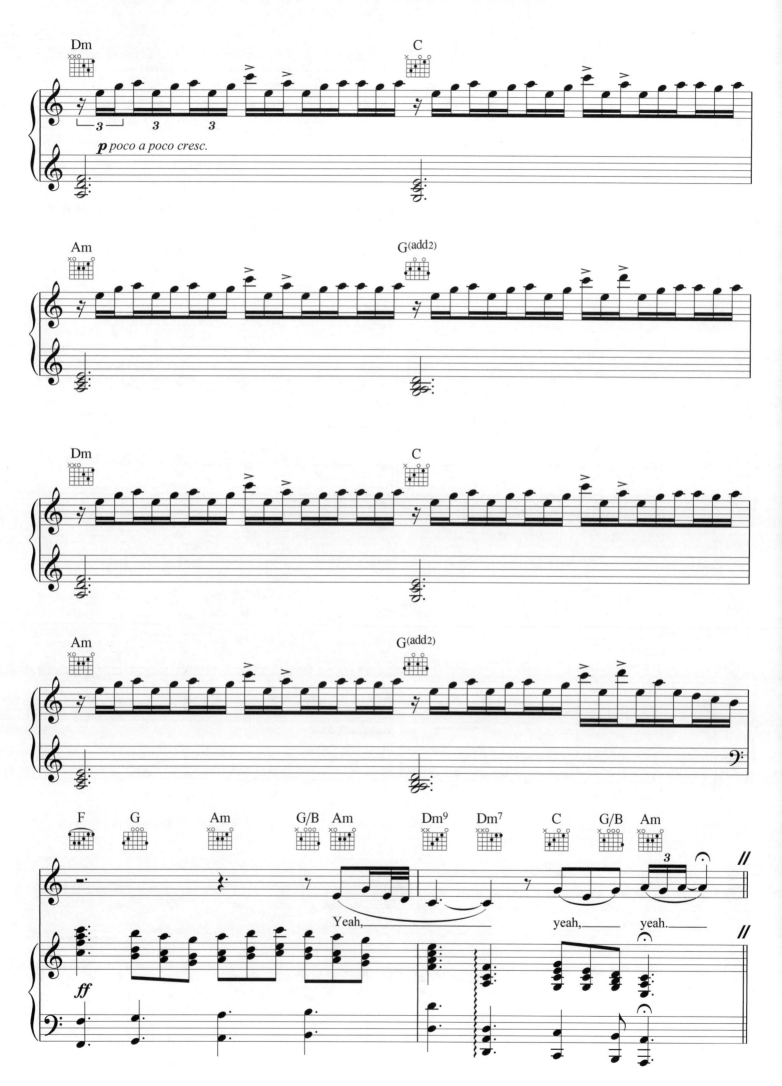

LISTEN

**WORDS & MUSIC BY BEYONCÉ KNOWLES,
HENRY KRIEGER, ANNE PREVEN & SCOTT CUTLER**

CD TRACK 4

© Copyright 2009 Famous Music Publishing Limited/Miroku Music Limited/B Day Publishing/Copyright Control.
EMI Music Publishing Limited (35%)/Sony/ATV Harmony (UK) Limited (16.66%)/Copyright Control (48.34%).
All Rights Reserved. International Copyright Secured.

NINE TO FIVE

WORDS & MUSIC BY DOLLY PARTON

© Copyright 1982 Velvet Apple Music, USA/Fox Fanfare Music Incorporated.
Carlin Music Corporation.
All Rights Reserved. International Copyright Secured.

ONLY HOPE
WORDS & MUSIC BY JONATHAN FOREMAN

PART OF YOUR WORLD

WORDS BY HOWARD ASHMAN
MUSIC BY ALAN MENKEN

THE WINNER TAKES IT ALL
WORDS & MUSIC BY BENNY ANDERSSON & BJÖRN ULVAEUS

Make a big impression with these song collections for auditions...

Audition Songs for Female Singers
Piano/vocal/guitar arrangements with CD backing tracks

Don't Cry For Me Argentina...
plus Adelaide's Lament, Big Spender; Heaven Help My Heart; I Cain't Say No; I Will Survive; Out Here On My Own; Saving All My Love For You; Someone To Watch Over Me; The Wind Beneath My Wings. ORDER NO. AM92587

I Dreamed A Dream...
plus Another Suitcase In Another Hall; Fame; If I Were A Bell; Miss Byrd; Save The Best For Last; Someone Else's Story; There Are Worse Things I Could Do; What I Did For Love; You Can Always Count On Me. ORDER NO. AM950224

Memory...
plus Can't Help Lovin' Dat Man; Crazy; Diamonds Are A Girl's Best Friend; Now That I've Seen Her; Show Me Heaven; That Ole Devil Called Love; The Winner Takes It All; Wishing You Were Somehow Here Again; The Reason. ORDER NO. AM955284

I Don't Know How To Love Him...
plus As Long As He Needs Me; Constant Craving; Feeling Good; I Say A Little Prayer; If My Friends Could See Me Now; It's Oh So Quiet; Killing Me Softly With His Song; Tell Me It's Not True; You Must Love Me. ORDER NO. AM955295

Beautiful...
plus Complicated; Don't Know Why; For What It's Worth; I'm Gonna Getcha Good!; Kiss Kiss; No More Drama; One Day I'll Fly Away; A Thousand Miles; Whenever, Wherever. ORDER NO. AM977130

Hits of the 90s
All Mine; Baby One More Time; Black Velvet; Chains; Don't Speak; From A Distance; Hero; Lovefool; Road Rage; What Can I Do. ORDER NO. AM966658

Blues
Cry Me A River; Black Coffee; Fine And Mellow (My Man Don't Love Me); The Lady Sings The Blues; Lover Man (Oh Where Can You Be); God Bless' The Child; Moonglow; Natural Blues; Please Send Me Someone To Love; Solitude. ORDER NO. AM966669

Classic Soul
Don't Make Me Over; I Just Want To Make Love To You; Midnight Train To Georgia; Nutbush City Limits; Private Number; Rescue Me; Respect; Son Of A Preacher Man; Stay With Me Baby; (Take A Little) Piece Of My Heart. ORDER NO. AM966670

R&B Hits
Ain't It Funny; AM To PM; Family Affair; Freak Like Me; Get The Party Started; How Come You Don't Call Me; Shoulda Woulda Coulda; Sweet Baby; Survivor; What About Us? ORDER NO. AM967351

Cabaret Songs
Big Spender; Cabaret; Falling In Love Again; I Am A Vamp; If My Friends Could See Me Now; The Ladies Who Lunch; Maybe This Time; Mein Herr; No Regrets (Non, Je Ne Regrette Rien); Take Me To Your Heart Again (La Vie En Rose). ORDER NO. AM958881

Classical Greats
Caro Mio Ben; Caro Nome; Habanera; Panis Angelicus; The Silver Swan; The Trout; Voi Che Sapete; When I Am Laid In Earth; Widmung; Wohin?. ORDER NO. AM984632

Number One Hits
American Pie; Can't Get You Out Of My Head; Don't Speak; Eternal Flame; Freak Like Me; I Will Always Love You; I Will Survive; Nothing Compares 2 U; The Winner Takes It All; A Woman In Love; plus ten more big songs (2 CDs). ORDER NO. AM91540

Audition Songs For Professional Singers
Black Velvet; Breathless; Emotion; From A Distance; Hero; History Repeating; My Love Is Your Love; Perfect Moment; Search For The Hero; That Don't Impress Me Much; Whole Again; plus 20 more top songs (2 CDs). ORDER NO. AM974578

Pop Hits For Professional Singers
Born To Try; The Closest Thing To Crazy; Don't Know Why; Hopelessly Devoted To You; I'm Gonna Getcha Good!; My Heart Will Go On; Son Of A Preacher Man; plus 20 more big hits (2 CDs). ORDER NO. AM90077

ALL TITLES AVAILABLE FROM GOOD MUSIC RETAILERS OR, IN CASE OF DIFFICULTY, CONTACT THE MARKETING DEPTARTMENT, MUSIC SALES LIMITED, NEWMARKET ROAD, BURY ST EDMUNDS, SUFFOLK IP33 3YB
marketing@musicsales.co.uk

CD TRACK LISTING

ANGEL *from* CITY OF ANGELS
SARAH MCLACHLAN
CD TRACK 1
(MCLACHLAN) SONY/ATV MUSIC PUBLISHING (UK) LIMITED

GOLDFINGER *from* GOLDFINGER
SHIRLEY BASSEY
CD TRACK 2
(BRICUSSE/NEWLEY/BARRY) SONY/ATV MUSIC PUBLISHING (UK) LIMITED

I'M KISSING YOU *from* ROMEO + JULIET
DES'REE
CD TRACK 3
(DES'REE/ATACK) SONY/ATV MUSIC PUBLISHING (UK) LIMITED/WESTBURY MUSIC CONSULTANTS LIMITED

LISTEN *from* DREAMGIRLS
BEYONCÉ
CD TRACK 4
(PREVEN/CUTLER/KRIEGER/KNOWLES) SONY/ATV HARMONY MUSIC (UK) LIMITED/EMI MUSIC PUBLISHING LIMITED/COPYRIGHT CONTROL

NINE TO FIVE *from* NINE TO FIVE
DOLLY PARTON
CD TRACK 5
(PARTON) CARLIN MUSIC CORPORATION

ONLY HOPE *from* A WALK TO REMEMBER
MANDY MOORE
CD TRACK 6
(FOREMAN) UNIVERSAL MUSIC PUBLISHING MGB LIMITED

PART OF YOUR WORLD *from* THE LITTLE MERMAID
JODI BENSON
CD TRACK 7
(ASHMAN/MENKEN) WARNER/CHAPPELL ARTEMIS MUSIC LIMITED

RUN TO YOU *from* THE BODYGUARD
WHITNEY HOUSTON
CD TRACK 8
(FRIEDMAN/RICH) PEERMUSIC (UK) LIMITED/UNIVERSAL/MCA MUSIC LIMITED

TAKE MY BREATH AWAY *from* TOP GUN
BERLIN
CD TRACK 9
(WHITLOCK/MORODER) SONY/ATV HARMONY MUSIC (UK) LIMITED/WARNER/CHAPPELL MUSIC NORTH AMERICA/GEMA

THE WINNER TAKES IT ALL *from* MAMMA MIA!
ABBA/MERYL STREEP
CD TRACK 10
(ANDERSSON/ULVAEUS) BOCU MUSIC LIMITED